THE APACHES

A First Americans Book

Virginia Driving Hawk Sneve

illustrated by Ronald Himler

Holiday House/New York

AUTHOR'S NOTE

The Apaches' creation story varies from tribe to tribe. The one used here is a combined retelling.

The information in this book barely touches on Apache history, culture, and present life. For more in-depth information on an individual Apache tribe, contact the specific Apache reservation.

The author would like to thank Merton Sandoval, Director of the Culture Preservation Program at the Jicarilla Apache Reservation, Jackie Tointigh of the Apache Tribe of Oklahoma, and the helpful staffs of The National Museum of the American Indian, the Bureau of Indian Affairs, and The American Museum of Natural History for their invaluable assistance and advice on this book.

Library of Congress Cataloging-in-Publication Data
Sneve, Virginia Driving Hawk.
The Apaches / Virginia Driving Hawk Sneve; illustrated by Ronald
Himler. — 1st. ed.
p.   cm. — (A First Americans book)
Includes bibliographical references and index.
Summary: Describes the social structure, daily life, religion,
government relations, and history of the Apache people.
ISBN 0-8234-1287-3 (library)
1. Apache Indians — History — Juvenile literature.   2. Apache
Indians — Social life and customs — Juvenile literature.   [1. Apache
Indians.   2. Indians of North America — New Mexico.]   I. Himler,
Ronald, ill.   II. Title.   III. Series: Sneve, Virginia Driving Hawk.
First Americans book.
E99.A6S63   1997   96-41358   CIP   AC
976'.004972 — dc20

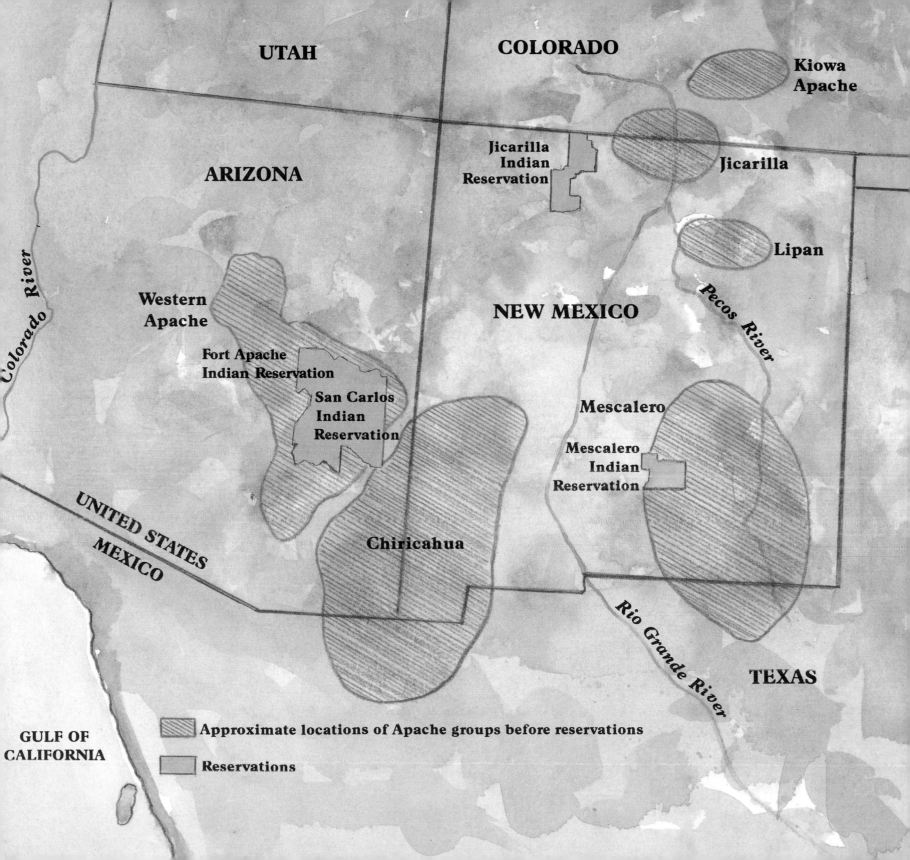

CREATION

On the beautiful mountains above it is daylight.

FROM A SONG OF GOTAL

In the beginning, Life Giver created the earth, but the earth was bare. Black Thunder made grasses and trees. Black Water caused streams and rivers to flow. Black Metal formed rocks and mountains, and Black Wind gave breezes to the earth.

Inside the earth, Life Giver created the sun and moon. Then he made the animals, birds, and people. At that time they could all talk to one another. But then the people and the other creatures quarreled with each other. This made Life Giver angry, and he let the sun and moon escape to the upper world. The people, animals, and birds followed the light.

After they had reached the outer world, Life Giver sent supernatural beings called *Gan* to teach the people how to live in a good way.

But the people found monsters who brought evil to the earth. Life Giver sent Changing Woman, a young girl, to the world. Changing Woman was also known as Painted Woman and White Shell Woman. She had two sons. The boys killed the monsters and made the earth safe for humans.

On earth, the animals and birds could no longer speak. But Life Giver allowed Coyote to behave like a human. Coyote then taught the people all of their customs.

4

HOMELAND

Be grateful for our land. It gives us all we have.
DILTH-CLEYHEN, DAUGHTER OF CHIEF VICTORIO

Chiricahua horned headdress

The people who emerged from the earth became known as Apache. The name might have come from the Zuni word *apachu,* which means "enemy." The Apaches call themselves *Tineh* or *Inde,* but both words mean "the people."

The Apaches were a nomadic tribe. Their traditional territory ranged from what is now New Mexico and Arizona through southeastern Colorado, western Oklahoma, much of Texas, and northern Mexico.

There were six Apache tribes: Chiricahua (cheer-acow-a), Jicarilla (hick-or-eea), Mescalero (Mez-caw-le-row), Kiowa-Apache (Ki-oh-wah), Lipan (Leh-pan), and Western Apache. The Mescaleros, Lipans, and Kiowa-Apaches were buffalo hunters who lived in teepees. The Comanches forced the Mescaleros from the buffalo ranges, but the Lipans and Kiowa-Apaches continued to live on the plains.

Each Apache tribe had cultural features that set it apart from the others, but they all had some customs in common. Although their languages were different, they could understand one other.

GOVERNMENT

We are all comrades, all one family, all one band.
GERONIMO

Apaches who followed the buffalo were teepee dwellers, while those who lived in the mountains had dome-shaped homes call wickiups. These structures were built using a framework made of branches, which was then covered with grass thatching or hides.

Families that were related lived in one place. A respected elderly man would act as the headman for this extended family, which came to be known by his name. A number of extended families who resided in the same general area made up a local group. The most dynamic family headman was acknowledged as the leader or "chief" of the local group. A chief led by his power to persuade. His authority extended only over the local group.

A local tribal group would stay in contact with groups from other areas so they could help one another in emergencies or to carry out tasks that required many people. When different tribal groups joined together in this way, they became known as bands. Different men would lead various band expeditions. There was never one single leader for a band, nor was there one single chief over all of the Apaches.

MEN

We want to live without danger and discomfort.
ALCHISAY

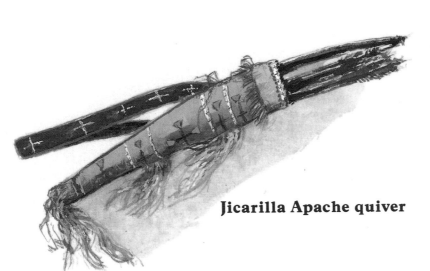

Jicarilla Apache quiver

man's shirt

After a man married, he provided for his wife's parents and obeyed their instructions. Only a few wealthy men could afford more than one wife because the husband had to support each wife's parents.

If a man's wife died, he was expected to provide for his in-laws for a year. If there were no eligible mates among his wife's relatives, the man could marry outside the family.

An Apache man hunted to provide food for his family. Often the men of an extended family hunted together. Sometimes a hunter wore a mask made from the head of a deer or antelope to lure the game closer. When the hunters brought game home, relatives shared the hide and meat.

Apache men had many other responsibilities. They went on raids to acquire horses. They fought to protect their families or avenge a relative's death. Many men were skilled trackers who could follow the faintest signs left by animals or humans.

Apache men once wore leather breechclouts and shirts, but after contact with the Spanish, they wore calico shirts. All wore moccasins and a headband to keep their long hair out of their eyes.

The men were skilled in using sign language to talk with people who spoke different languages. They arranged their hands and fingers in certain positions or signs which had special meanings. They also communicated over great distances by flashing sun rays on mirrors, or arranging fires in patterns, or sending smoke signals.

An Apache man could become chief of his local group if he was a skilled hunter and warrior. But he also had to be trusted by the others in the group before he became its leader.

WOMEN

Be strong! For you are the mother of a people.
FROM A MESCALERO SONG OF
THE GIRLS' PUBERTY CEREMONY

**seed beater
and basket**

**woman's
buckskin dress**

The Apaches believed that their women were the mainstays of the people. The men respected, cherished, and protected the women. After marriage, a man moved to his wife's home. If a woman's husband died, she was asked to marry his unmarried brother or cousin.

Apache women cared for their children and helped one another in many tasks.

Women of most Apache tribes gathered seeds, berries, roots, and nuts to feed their families. These were either eaten fresh, mixed with meat, or dried. The women worked together to prepare food. They fried, broiled, or boiled meat they planned to eat right away. They dried some meat to preserve for future meals.

Women of some tribes planted corn, melons, pumpkins, squash, beans, onions, and potatoes. But most of the tribes relied on hunting and gathering for their food.

Women also helped one another build teepees and wickiups and tan and sew hides for the buckskin clothes and moccasins their families wore. After contact with whites, the women gave up their buckskin dresses and donned long, full cotton skirts and hip-length blouses, but they continued to wear bootlike moccasins with turned-up toes. Sometimes the women beaded or painted the moccasins. Men and children wore similar footwear.

Apache women often wore necklaces made of shell, glass, or bean beads. They wore shell earrings and brass or silver bracelets.

The women made gathering and storage baskets. Some were waterproofed with piñon pitch to hold liquids. The Jicarillas, whose name means "little basket," became known for their basketry.

awl and its case

hide scraper

burden basket

woman's buckskin moccasins

waterproof water jar

13

century plant
(Agave americana)

mescal
knife

mescal crown

digging stick

Mescal, also known as agave or century plant, was a favorite food. In fact the name Mescalero means "mescal people." Apache women picked tender mescal shoots to roast. They dug the crowns and trimmed and baked them in pits. The baked agave was then sun-dried and stored to be a staple food supply for many months.

CHILDREN

When my songs were first heard, the holy mountain was standing toward me with life.

FROM A WHITE MOUNTAIN SONG OF THE GIRLS' PUBERTY CEREMONY

cradleboard

child's moccasins

child's doll

Every Apache baby was placed in a cradleboard made especially for that infant. An ornament, or amulet, would be hung on the cradleboard to protect the child from evil. The mother or grandmother pierced the baby's earlobes so the child would hear the right things and obey.

When a child was ready to walk, the Mescalero, a "putting-on-moccasins" ceremony, was held. The boy or girl was dressed in new clothes and moccasins. He or she walked to the east on a trail of pollen. A medicine man prayed that the child would have a long and successful journey through life. The following spring a haircutting rite took place. Only a few tufts of hair were left to encourage new hair to grow. This would ensure that the child had good health as he or she became older.

Both boys and girls were trained to rise early, to run often, and to do strenuous tasks in order to become physically fit.

Boys were trained for the hardships of raiding and war. They ran, wrestled, had mock fights, and learned to play the hoop and pole game, which was a game for men and boys. Two players would try to roll the hoop to a designated spot so that it would fall over the end of the pole. The game required a player to be skillful and quick.

hoop and pole game

A boy learned by listening to his father or grandfather tell stories of his experiences in hunting or war. He also heard tales of the historic deeds of the Apaches. In addition, a grandfather taught a boy both how he should behave on a hunt and different methods of killing game.

A grandfather also taught chants and prayers that were used during hunting ceremonies. He helped his grandson make a bow and arrows, then he showed the boy how to use the weapons, and made him practice until he became a skilled marksman. Later, the boy was allowed to go on his first hunt.

When a boy was about twelve or thirteen he was permitted to go with the men on a raid to get horses. He was to behave as he had been taught and stay out of the way. Boys learned a special vocabulary that was used only on raids and in warfare. If a boy acted properly on his first four raids, he was thought to be a man.

Apache girls were also taught how to use a bow and arrows and how to ride horses. They also learned by helping their mothers and other women tan and sew, gather food and firewood, and care for younger children. The girls helped older female relatives when they cooked and built wickiups.

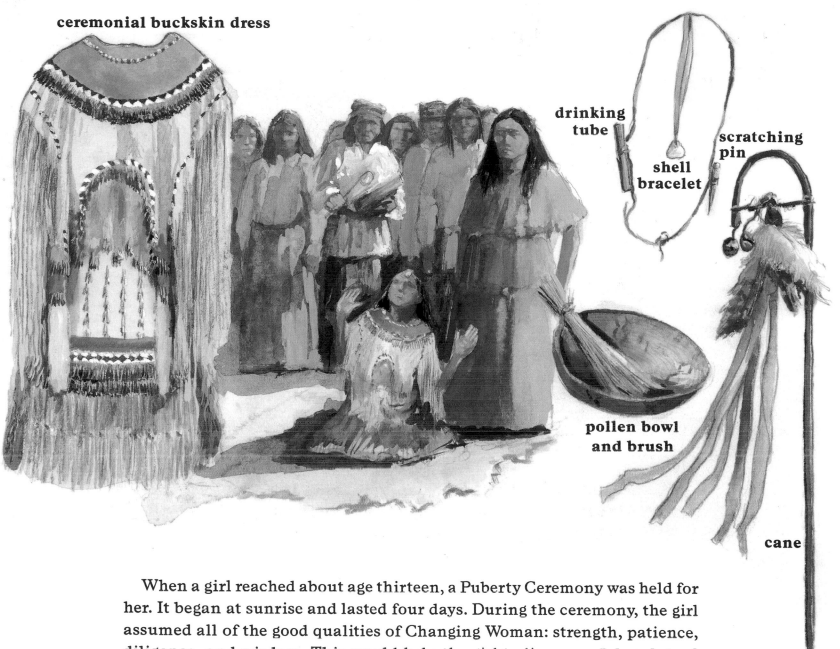

ceremonial buckskin dress

drinking tube

shell bracelet

scratching pin

pollen bowl and brush

cane

When a girl reached about age thirteen, a Puberty Ceremony was held for her. It began at sunrise and lasted four days. During the ceremony, the girl assumed all of the good qualities of Changing Woman: strength, patience, diligence, and wisdom. This would help the girl to live a useful and good life.

When boys and girls were old enough to marry, a boy's relatives gave presents to the girl's family. If they accepted the gifts, the marriage took place. The girl's female relatives built the couple a new wickiup near the bride's parents.

CEREMONY

The power of these mountains is power you can't explain.
MELFERD YUZOS, SR.

Gan mask

The Apaches' religion was not separate from the rest of their lives. They believed that a great power was in the universe. Humans could acquire part of this power, but a person had to learn how to use this power in the correct way. This was done by always remembering its presence and learning the songs and prayers that went with it.

If a person had evil power, he or she was a witch who could make people ill or cause misfortune. Apache medicine men held curing ceremonies to expel the evil.

The plains Apache held summer ceremonies to seek power for successful buffalo hunts. The mountain Apaches held a ceremony in which the men wore spirit masks representing the Mountain Spirits or *Gan*. These men were called Masked Dancers or Crown Dancers. This ceremony was done to cure certain sicknesses. Pollen was often used in such ceremonies because it represented growth and vitality.

Some Apache tribes had ceremonial races in the fall to celebrate the harvest and long life.

RAIDING AND WAR

*If somebody's coming into your house to take it,
you wouldn't stand for it.*

ALLAN HOUSER

buffalo horned headdress

war lance

The Apaches believed there was a difference between going on a raid and going to war. The purpose of a raid was to acquire horses or other livestock. During a raid the men avoided contact with the enemy. If the raiders were discovered, they would have to fight. But it was more important for them to escape with horses without any injuries or deaths. The purpose of a war, however, was to avenge the deaths of tribe members killed by enemies. The family of the slain led these wars, and their chief invited relatives from other groups to join the battle.

If possible, the Apaches tried to go after the actual killer, but if this was not possible, they would attack the nearest town, settlement, or village in the enemy's territory.

After a battle, the warriors scattered to meet at a prearranged site.

THE COMING OF THE WHITE MEN

We believed your assurances of friendship, and we trusted them.

MANGAS COLORADAS

Alchisay

In 1540 Francisco de Coronado explored what is now southeastern Arizona. He reported seeing a tribe now believed to be Apaches. The Apaches watched these new people settle among the Pueblo tribes. The Spaniards brought horses, and the Apaches soon learned to use the animal. They began raiding Spanish missions and settlements to get horses.

The Spaniards made some of the southwestern tribes settle at their missions and work for them, but the Apaches would not stay in one place. While the usual Spanish policy was to kill Apaches, some Spanish commanders tried to make peace with them.

In 1786 the viceroy of New Spain began a new way of dealing with the Apaches. He made agreements with those who promised to settle at military posts. The Apaches who refused to come in were searched out and killed.

The Spaniards gave the Apaches who came in corn, beans, tobacco, sugar, and cattle. Later the Apaches asked for guns to use for hunting. Some of these Apache men became scouts for the Spaniards.

Because the Apaches lived near the Spaniards, they were exposed to the white man's diseases. Many Apaches died of smallpox and other illnesses for which they had no immunity.

In 1824 Mexico became independent, and the peace with the Apaches ended. The Apaches began raiding, and the Mexican government set a bounty on Apache scalps of 100 pesos for a man's and 50 for a woman's or child's. In response, the Apaches began to scalp their dead enemies.

After the 1848 Treaty of Guadalupe Hidalgo ending the Mexican War, much of present-day Arizona and New Mexico became part of the United States. Now the Apaches were under the control of the U.S. government.

American miners and settlers began moving through Apache territory. They wanted the government to protect them from the Indians. The Apaches called the Americans "white eyes" because many had light-colored eyes.

There were frequent clashes between whites and Apaches. Forts were built in Arizona to guard settlements and routes to the gold fields.

In 1855 the U.S. Congress approved money to move the Chiricahuas to one area where they could be kept away from the whites.

**flop head
war club**

Cochise

Michael Steck, a government agent, met with the Chiricahuas near Apache Pass and persuaded them not to attack immigrants on the overland trail. The Indians kept their word until Cochise and four other headmen were tricked and arrested. Cochise cut his way through a tent and escaped, but the others were executed. Cochise then took revenge by attacking any whites who used Apache Pass.

After the U.S. Civil War began, Union troops were pulled out of the area. New Mexico Territory was invaded by Confederates from Texas. In 1862 U.S. troops from California, led by General James H. Carleton, regained New Mexico from the Confederates. Carleton's policy was to confine the Apaches to one place.

RESERVATIONS

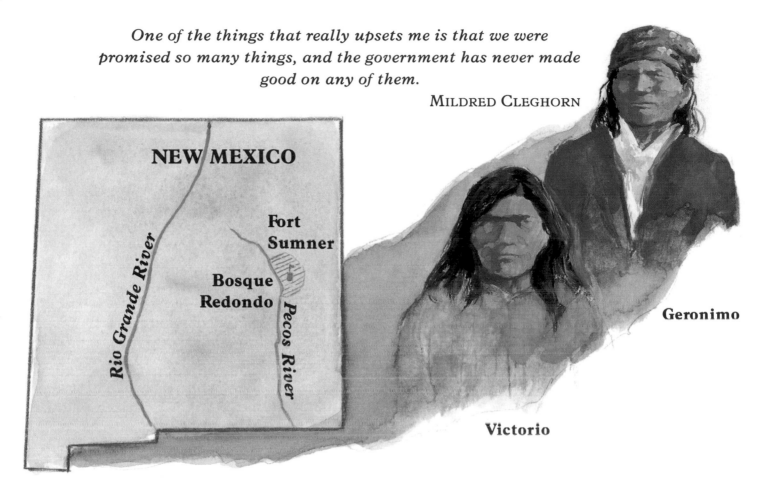

One of the things that really upsets me is that we were promised so many things, and the government has never made good on any of them.

MILDRED CLEGHORN

NEW MEXICO

Fort Sumner

Bosque Redondo

Rio Grande River

Pecos River

Victorio

Geronimo

The Apaches fiercely resisted reservation settlement until they were finally forced to surrender.

In November 1862 General Carleton ordered the establishment of a reservation on the Pecos River near Fort Sumner. It was known as Bosque Redondo. The Mescalero Apaches and Navajos were settled there. The reservation had bad drinking water, little fuel, and poor land. The Indians were hungry, unhappy, and angry. Fights broke out between the Navajos and Apaches. By 1868 most of the Apaches had fled the reservation.

In the 1870s the U.S. government decided that all Apaches should be placed on reservations. General George Crook was ordered to "tame" them. He ordered the Apaches to "come to the reservation or die." Crook hired Apache men as scouts because they knew the land and could guide the army to hideouts in the mountains.

In 1876 the San Carlos Reservation was created by the government, which ordered the Chiricahuas to move there. After the Indians arrived, they realized they did not like the place and hated being confined. Goyathlay (also known as Geronimo) and Victorio decided to leave, and many of the Chiricahuas followed them out of the reservation.

In the summer of 1886, General Nelson A. Miles took 5,000 soldiers and Apache scouts after Geronimo. On September 4, 1886, Geronimo and his followers surrendered. They and all of the San Carlos Chiricahuas were imprisoned at Fort Marion, Florida. Even those who had never left the reservation and those who had served as U.S. Army scouts were sent to Florida.

By the end of 1889, 119 of the 498 Chiricahuas in Florida had died of disease. In 1894 all were moved to a reservation at Fort Sill, Oklahoma.

In 1912 the Chiricahuas were given a choice of accepting land near Fort Sill or going south to share a reservation with the Mescaleros. Of the 271 Chiricahuas at Fort Sill, 187 decided to return to the mountains of the southwest, while 84 stayed in Oklahoma.

Eventually all of the Apache tribes were assigned to reservations.

Texas settlers drove the Lipans into Mexico where they were slaughtered by Mexican troops. The few dozens who survived later found a home with the Mescaleros.

On some Apache reservations, people were identified by number and not by name. All married men were assigned numbers, and their wives took the same number. The Apaches were given numbered metal tags on bands to wear around their necks. Girls used their fathers' tags until they married. Boys had their own tag bands. This practice lasted until 1913.

Victorio's band was driven into Mexico by U.S. forces. On October 15, 1880, Victorio and most of his followers were killed in a battle with Mexican soldiers.

war charm necklace

TODAY

We're going to survive; we're going to make it.
BERLE KANSEAH

There are more than 50,000 Apaches in the United States. Most of them live on reservations in Arizona and New Mexico.

Children attend school on and off reservations. Many Apaches are college graduates and work as lawyers, doctors, teachers, and in other professional occupations. Other Apaches are farmers, ranchers, and businessmen.

Some make beautiful baskets and other crafts. The works of Apache artist Allan Houser have become world famous.

Some tribes operate successful ranching, forestry, tourism, and gambling businesses which employ hundreds of Apaches. Others work for their tribe's hunting, fishing, and skiing enterprises.

Although the Apaches lost their lands, freedom, and culture, they are an important part of American history. Even today they continue to value ancient traditions and ceremonies. The Girls' Puberty Ceremony and the Mountain Spirit Ceremony are still important to them.

When I was young I walked all over this country, east and west, and saw no other people than the Apaches. After many summers I walked again and found another race of people had come to take it . . .

I want to live in these mountains . . . I have drunk of these waters and they have cooled me; I do not want to leave here.

COCHISE

Apache fiddle and drum

APACHE TRIBES TODAY

The Apache Tribe of Oklahoma, Anadarko, Oklahoma (Kiowa-Apache)

Camp Verde Yavapai-Apache Reservation, Camp Verde, Arizona

Fort McDowell Mohave-Apache Indian Community of the Fort McDowell Reservation, Fountain Hills, Arizona (Yavapai, Mohave, and Apache)

Fort Sill Apache Tribe of Oklahoma, Apache, Oklahoma

Jicarilla Apache Tribe of the Jicarilla Reservation, Dulce, New Mexico

Mescalero Apache Tribe of the Mescalero Reservation, Mescalero, New Mexico. The Lipan or Tcicihi Apaches also live here.

San Carlos Apache Tribe of the San Carlos Reservation, San Carlos, Arizona

Tonto Apache Tribe of Arizona, Tonto Reservation, Payson, Arizona

White Mountain Apache Tribe of the Fort Apache Reservation, Whiteriver, Arizona

ACKNOWLEDGMENTS

All of the quotations used in this book are from Apache people.

The quote from "A Song of Gotal" is from *The Sky Clears: Poetry of the American Indian.* (Lincoln: University of Nebraska Press, 1964 rpt).

The Dilth-cleyhen quote is from *The Woman's Way.* (Alexandria, VA: Time-Life Books, 1995).

The Geronimo and Alchisay quotes are from *The Way: Anthology of American Indian Literature,* Shirley Hill Witt and Stan Steiner, eds. (New York: Alfred A. Knopf, 1974).

The quotes of Mangas Coloradas and Cochise are reprinted from *I Have Spoken: American History Through the Voices of the Indians,* Virginia Irving Armstrong, ed. (Athens: Ohio University Press/Swallow Press, 1971).

The quotes from the Mescalero and White Mountain songs of the Girls' Puberty Ceremony are from *The Sacred Path: Spells, Prayers & Power Songs of the American Indians,* John Bierhorst, ed. (New York: William Morrow, 1983).

The Melferd Yuzos, Sr., Allan Houser, and Berle Kanseah quotes are from "Geronimo and the Apache Resistance," *The American Experience.* (Alexandria, VA: PBS Home Video, Pacific Arts, 1989).

Mildred Cleghorn's quote is from *The Book of Elders: The Life Stories & Wisdom of Great American Indians,* Sandy Johnson and Dan Budnik, eds. Text copyright © 1994 by Sandy Johnson. Photographs copyright © 1994 by Dan Budnik. Reprinted by permission of Harper Collins, Inc.

INDEX

Alchisay, 9, 22
Apaches
  creation stories of, 2, 4
  government of, 8
  origins, 6
  Spanish and, 10, 22–23
  white men and, 13, 22–24

Bosque Redondo, 25

Carleton, General James H., 24, 25
century plant, *see* mescal
Changing Woman, 4, 17
children, 15–17
Chiricahua, 3, 6, 23, 24, 26, 27
Civil War, 24
clothing, 9, 10, 12, 13, 15
Cochise, 24, 29
Comanches, 6
Coronado, Francisco de, 22
cradleboard, 15
Crook, General George, 26
Crown Dancers, 18

disease, 23

Fort Apache Reservation, 3, 30
Fort Marion, 27
Fort Sill, 27, 30
Fort Sumner, 25

games, 15–16
Gan, 4, 18
Geronimo, 8, 25, 26, 27
Goyathlay, *see* Geronimo

horses, 22
Houser, Allan, 20, 28
hunting, 9, 12, 16

Jicarilla, 3, 6, 9, 13, 30

Kiowa-Apache, 3, 6, 30

language, 6, 10
Lipan, 3, 6, 27, 30

Masked Dancers, *see* Crown
  Dancers
men, roles of, 9–11
mescal, 14
Mescalero, 3, 6, 12, 14, 25, 27, 30
Mescalero Ceremony, 15
Miles, General Nelson A., 27
moccasins, 10, 13, 15

Navajos, 25

Puberty Ceremony, 12, 15, 17, 28
putting-on-moccasins ceremony, *see*
  Mescalero Ceremony

raids, 9, 15, 16, 20–21, 22, 23
reservations, 3, 25–27, 28, 30

San Carlos Reservation, 3, 26, 27, 30
scalping, 23
Steck, Michael, 24

teepees, 6, 8
Treaty of Guadalupe Hidalgo, 23

Victorio, 6, 25, 26

wickiups, 6, 8, 13, 16, 17
women, roles of, 12–14

Zuni, 6